Y0-CYF-477

*To all who
have helped carry
Her name forward
to our time.*

Dearest Goddess
Copyright © 1985 by Eso Benjamins
First Edition

All rights reserved. Printed in the United States of America. No part of this book may be used or reproduced in any manner whatsoever without written permission, except in the case of brief quotations embodied in critical articles or reviews. For information address Current Nine Publishing, P.O. Box 6089, Arlington, VA 22206.

Library of Congress Catalog Card Number: 85-72555

ISBN 0-9615413-1-8

Published by Current Nine Publishing
Manufactured in the United States of America
First Edition: October 1985

Dearest Goddess

Translations from Latvian Folk Poetry

by Eso Benjamins

Current Nine Publishing

Many thanks to my wife, Cynthia Reddy Benjamins, without whose help and encouragement it would have been so much more difficult to complete the work.

CONTENTS

INTRODUCTION

Who is the Dearest Goddess*?*
In ancient Latvia on the Baltic sea, she is the sun. According to the Latvian way of thinking, the sun provides not only warmth and the colors of the rainbow, but good as well.

The Dearest Goddess may also be visualized as walking a country road in a colorful folk costume. Latvian women were great weavers and wore their best not only as personal adornment, but to suggest what the Dearest Goddess might look like if she were to be seen walking a country path, or crossing a farm yard, or a village street. It is not uncommon to hear Latvians refer to women in folk costumes as "the daughters of the sun".

If the Dearest Goddess was the Sun, was she the feminine equal to God?

No doubt, in some parts of the world the Dearest Goddess was more important than God, but her preeminence was undermined when war elevated men and arms. This is, more or less, what happened to the Latvians. When war overtook their region and brought with it Christianity, the image of the nurturing feminine sun was replaced by a male God.

It is fortunate that most Latvian folk songs or dainas—*of which there are over a million collected examples—were created, for the most part (80 percent), by Latvian women. The* dainas *give evidence that once away from the Christian church, Latvian women continued to address their own Dearest Goddess.*

The following translations are evidence of that practice.

* * *

A word about the translation.
The Latvian language, strongly influenced and shaped by a feminine psyche, can turn most words into an endearment, also known as a diminutive. *The endearing word is used frequently by*

the Latvian dainas, *sometimes two or three times in a short stanza. Because the user of diminutives assumes the listener has a native's familiarity with the environment, such a poem can become extremely subjective. A short cut to poetry for Latvians, the endearment remains one of the chief obstacles to translating Latvian* dainas. *It is one of the reasons why these poems remain so little known.*

In order to overcome this and other problems of translation, I have sometimes used the "agglomeration and selection" method. That is, I have scanned two, sometimes three or more dainas *in order to discover appropriate images for the English language.*

The archive numbers of the dainas *are included for those who wish to refer to the source.*

The Dearest Goddess is known as Laima *in Latvian.*

—Eso Benjamins
1985

Latvian Folk Poetry

I HAVE LOOKED...

8617. 190.
8631. 206.

I have looked
for her
here,
there,
everywhere,
but
my Dearest Goddess
is playing
games
with me:

She will not
tell me
where
I can
find her.
She's making
me spin
in my
chair.

I'LL TELL YOU...

8467. 111.

I'll tell you
why I
divorced
my first
husband:

He praised me
to heaven,
but seldom
took me
to bed.

Dearest Goddess,
I was so furious,
I could have let
the devil
tear
his heart out.

MY LOVER...

8453. 60.
8454. 181.

My lover
wishes
to cheat
on me.
He says
he will lead me
to the blue blossoms
of an apple tree.

Dearest Goddess,
I know
that apple blossoms
are white.
I'm not going to
be the fool
to follow
a fool,
and
let him
rob me
of the self-esteem
you gave me.

YOU BET...

8794. 3.
8806. 181.
40547. 213.

You bet
jealousy
will not
hinder me.

Your words,
along with you,
will fall
into
the abyss.

You see,
it so happens
the Dearest Goddess
is sitting
in my
rose garden
with me.

YOU WILL...

9015. 217.
9050. 337.
9118. 73.

You will never
find me
among
the chaff.

The Dearest Goddess
leads me;
with Dearest God
my Dearest Goddess
will lift me
up to
the mountain top.

DO YOU SEE...

50645. 294.

Dearest Goddess,
do you see
all that
blue smoke
at the edge
of the forest?

That is where
there is
a fiery pit
for the carcass
of the man
who fools me.

DEAREST GODDESS...

9160. 88.

Dearest Goddess,
why were
you looking
the other way
when I
was born?

Why did you
make me
so squat?
Why did you
give me
a bony head?
What am I
to do
with
these large
hands
and feet?

OH DEAREST GOD...

9158[1]. 131[1].

Oh Dearest God,
what's
going to happen
now?
Is it true?
My heart aches.

Is
the Dearest Goddess
dead
there
at the bottom
of the deep
rock pit?

IS THE DEAREST GODDESS...

9163. 88.

Is the Dearest Goddess
a cuck-coo bird?

This one gives
to some
too much,
while
others have
nothing
at all.

IF YOU DON'T...

9167. 52.

If you don't
stop crying
you will drown
the Dearest Goddess.

See!
Already
your puddle
of tears
is rising
into
a tide.

I FLED...

9170. 120.

I fled
from myself
day and
night
and almost
escaped me.

I cannot
escape
the Dearest Goddess
though.
She
has been telling
my life
from
my birthday
on.

JUST THINK...

9172. 134.

Just think
of it,
Dearest Goddess!

Though
you made
my childhood years
so difficult,
that
does not mean
I should
not be
happy
today.

KEEP ME...

9176. 157.

Give me
health,
Dearest Goddess.
It will
keep me
singing
and help weaken
evil
days.

YOU GO FIRST...

9180. 6, 68,
88, 305, 345.

You go first,
Dearest Goddess.
I'll follow
in your
footsteps.
Don't let
me step
into
evil days.

LET US EAT...

6038 (19460)

Let us eat
let us drink,
let us say
thanks
to Dearest God
and Goddess.

It is
the God's bread,
it is
the Goddess's
table,
it is reward
for
my own
hard labor.

DEAREST GODDESS...

6533 (21733)
6653 (22177)

Dearest Goddess,
my man's
so tough
all he needs
is a sword
to become
a warrior
and make me
a widow
—a mother
to orphans.

IS IT...

6671 (22223)
6676 (22237)

Is it
the decision
of Dearest God?
Is it
the wish
of the Dearest Goddess?
Yesterday
I was
a beekeeper's daughter
melting wax.
Today
my heart melts
for the man
in the smithy.

SUCH...

5674 (18304)

Such
is my
marriage
ceremony:
First,
I cut
a cross,
then give
him
my hand.

May the sun
always
be before us,
may the Dearest Goddess
always follow
in our
footsteps.

LOOK,...

5724 (18471)

Look,
Dearest Goddess,
here comes
the fisherman's
bride.

On her head
she wears
a herring
skeleton
crown.
In her train
follows
a dance
of flies.

LET...

5837 (18826)

Let
the sword
cut a cross
in our door.
Let it
cut out
the devil,
the Unwelcome Goddess,
and jealousy;
but let in
the Dearest Goddess.

WHAT SHALL...

6019 (19391)

What shall
we do,
Dearest Goddess,
with Liz?
She's
the witch's
daughter.
She's the first
to reach
for butter.
She can eat
a barrel
full
of oatmeal
all by herself.

WHAT WILL HAPPEN...

11709. 115. 131.

What will happen,
Dearest Goddess,
if the man
doesn't
come dancing
and dies
a bachelor?

I'll tell you.
For five years
a devil
will dance
on his grave.
For three years
the rats
will chew
on his boots.

MAY THOSE BOYS...

12234. 88.

May those boys
go to
the devil
croaking
like frogs.
May these girls
go to
the Dearest Goddess
blooming
like cherry
trees.

PROTECT...

41937. 50

Protect,
Dearest Goddess,
the young men
from these
three
unwelcome traits:

steeling,
and lying,
and cheating
on young girls.

THE DEAREST GODDESS...

12001. 270.

The Dearest Goddess
sits spinning
her strands
on the mountain
top.
Will she
mate me
with an ass?
Or will it be
the man
I want?

THIS...

41846. 399.
41607. 200

This,
Dearest Goddess,
is what
you gave me
to brag about:
hard tits,
a long neck,
and
a pug nose.
It's
all mine.

THE BRIDEGROOM...

42045. 192.   The bridegroom
                      is bragging,
                      he claims
                      to have taken
                      a bride
                      as polished
                      as a
                      linden board.

                      The Dearest Goddess
                      will tell him
                      the truth:
                      the bride
                      is as rough
                      as a board
                      hewn
                      with an axe.

EVEN THOUGH...

35914. 389.

Even though
I've tried
singing
and crying,
my Dearest Goddess
will not come
and speak
with me.
Has she
fallen asleep?
Does she
no longer
care
about me?

I'M OUT...

35806. 398.

I'm out
of songs,
Dearest Goddess.
What shall
I do?

I know.
Let me find
an old bachelor.
Let me
ride him
to find
a new song.

HERE I AM...

11397. 6.

Here I am
imagining
for myself
a rich bride.

What good
is imagination
if
the Dearest Goddess
decides
otherwise?

THE BRAGGARD...

11721. 75.
11722. 73.

The braggard
is claiming
he'll soon
find
for himself
a bride.

Says
the Dearest Goddess:
what's
your claim?
Where are
your good habits?
Your breath
stinks of booze.
Haven't you
been rolling
in ashes?

DANCE, MARSHA...

11696. 324.   Dance, Marsha,
dance.
Take
no worry.
Your Dearest Goddess
guards you.
Your Dearest Goddess
sits
in a silver boat
and wears
a golden
crown.

THIS MILL...

7926. 311.

This mill
is too much;
the wheel
is too heavy.
Dearest Goddess,
it's been
a hard life.
I no longer
wish
to keep walking
in circles.

WE'RE OUT OF...

8243. 302.

We're out
of bread,
Dearest Goddess.
Where shall
we find
a new loaf?

Give us
your keys,
Dearest Goddess.
We'll go
look
for new flour
in Dearest God's
grainery.

I'VE HAD ENOUGH...

9167. 52.

I've had enough,
Dearest Goddess,
listening
to evil tongues.
I wish them
the devil
in their hearts,
a horn
on their foreheads,
and a pimple
on the tip
of their tongues.

COME...

3462 (1197)

Come,
be my guest,
Dearest Goddess.
I'll give you
an easy chair
to sit in.
Then I am
going
to wait
for you
to declare
easy days
for me.

SOME PEOPLE...

9227. 278. 21.

Some people
are saying
that
my Dearest Goddess
has died
by drowning.
Well,
I just saw her
walking
over
the waters
sowing
handfulls
of gold
and silver.

BECAUSE...

35889. 476.
35892. 418.

Dearest Goddess,
because
it makes you
glad,
I will go
through life
singing.

If I cry,
I make happy
only
evil days.

DEAREST GODDESS...

9188. 224. 109.
9188. 335.

Dearest Goddess,
if you are
going to meet
the Unwelcome Goddess,
why not meet her
on the bridge?
I will walk by
and push
the Unwelcome Goddess
into
the river.

WHAT MAKES...

9196. 68.
9198. 111.

What makes you,
Dearest Goddess,
lead me
such
a difficult
life?
When I
stand up,
I cry;
when I walk,
I pour
perspiration.

I ASKED...

9236. 264.
9242. 407.

I asked of
Dearest God
good health,
of
my Dearest Goddess
a good life.
Here's
what happened:
God
teased, and reversed
the order.
He wished me
a good life.
The Dearest Goddess,
grew angry
and said
God's in the wrong
and it's not
my due.

WHAT SHALL I...

40550. 605.

What shall I do,
Dearest God?
The Dearest Goddess
has drowned.
Shall I jump
into the sea
and save her?

GIVE ME...

7894. 198.
39945. 292.
39930. 195.

Give me
a rich man,
Dearest Goddess.
My savings
are gone.
This morning
I found
a mouse
with a broken neck
at the bottom
of my
piggy bank.

WHY,...

40553. 127.

Why,
Dearest Goddess,
did you
make me
so short?
Every time
it rains
my hair
gets wet
in the grass.

IF YOU STRETCH...

40586. 146.

If you stretch
a hand
for her,
she'll come
to give you
her own.
If you wish
to give her
a kick,
you may
be sure
the Dearest Goddess
will never
come near
you.

HELP ME...

3467 (1211)
3468 (1223)

Help me,
Dearest Goddess,
Dearest God,
help
a poor orphan.
Give me,
Dearest Goddess,
a long life.
Let me see,
Dearest God,
only good.

DEAREST GOD...

5493 (17772)

Dearest God,
I like
your laws;
Dearest Goddess,
I like
your decisions:

two strangers
meet
and live
their lives
together
in peace.

THIS IS...

3470 (1228)

This is
some birthing place
you have,
Dearest Goddess.
My hair
becomes
all matted
the moment
I walk
in.

I SAID...

3475 (1249)

I said
I would not
grow old.
Years later
I met
the Dearest Goddess.
I should
have known...
I had stepped
into
an old woman's
footsteps.

I COULD NOT...

3476 (1256)

I could not
sleep
last night.
Last night
the Dearest Goddess
and I
sat together
and talked
for a
long time.

LET US BOTH...

3799 (1987)
3787 (1955)

Let us both
think,
Dearest Goddess.
If the child
is a son,
he'll become
a soldier.
Should I
throw him
into the river?
If the child
is a daughter
she'll sing us
sweet songs.

DON'T FORBID...

4525 (15297)

Don't forbid me,
mother,
my first love,
my true love.
The Dearest Goddess
is here
with us.

WHEN OUT...

5377 (17427)

When out
walking
I met
my Dearest Goddess
and found
her thinking.
Being wise
I stopped
and waited
to find out
what she
thought.

I HAVE...

4200 (14264)

I have
an outrageous
sister:
she even tried
outsmarting
Dearest God.
Or was it
the Dearest Goddess
who whispered to her
that she could
marry
her sister's man?

THEY'RE ALL...

42126. 281.

They're all
saying,
I'm sitting,
I'm sitting,
I'm sitting.

Dearest Goddess
knows,
I'm sitting
only
until
she makes
me do.

ALAS,...

13854. 293.

Alas,
even
an evil man
prays
to God
and the Dearest Goddess,
alas,
to fool
a good woman
into becoming
his wife.

WHAT HAPPENED...

12683. 182.

What happened,
Dearest Goddess,
to my
dozen lovers?

Three hung themselves,
Three shot themselves,
Three went to retire.
It will take
a log
to lever
the remaining three
out of
my bed.

GOOD MORNING...

42976. 378.

Good morning,
Dearest Goddess.
Have you seen
my bride?

Yes.
She's on
the other side
of the river
in a wild patch
of blooming
roses.

I'M NOT WORRIED...

13225. 174.
13232. 88.

Dearest Goddess,
I have
all the time
in the world.
I even
have time
to tie
my shoes
while sitting
in bed
on my pillow.

I SEE YOU...

33661. 229.

I see you
sowing silver,
Dearest Goddess,
all around
the seashore.
Sow,
Dearest Goddess,
a share
for me.
An acre
or two
will do.

WHO WILL OPEN...

54628. 241.

Who will open
the gates?
Who will open
the door
of the house
for me?

Dearest God
will come
to open the gates.
The Dearest Goddess
will invite me
into
the house.

GOD WALKS...

54647. 114.

God walks
across the fields
of wheat.
He's wearing
a grey coat
and brings
the rain.

The Dearest Goddess
comes
walking behind
and sows
the golden petals
of sunshine.

ALL'S WELL...

54639. 326.   All's well,
                 all's well.
                 God
                 has put egg
                 in my porridge.
                 All's well,
                 all's well.
                 The Dearest Goddess
                 adds yeast
                 and honey.

WHO OWNS...

54696. 572.

Who owns
the house
with three gates?

The Dearest Goddess
and God
enter
through the first
two gates.
The third gate
belongs
to the sun.

IF YOU'RE SAD...

54798. 389.

If you're sad,
dear brother,
go climb
the mountain.
There
the Dearest Goddess
will speak
to you
with
your mother's
sweet words.

DEAR SISTER...

54802. 604.

Dear sister,
this is
the place
where
two hostesses
will come
to greet you.

The Dearest Goddess
will untie
your shoes
and set
the table.
The other,
the Sun,
will unsaddle
your horse.

WHOSE...

54814. 170

Whose steeds
of wind
prance
before
the church door?

They belong to
the Dearest Goddess
in the golden
carriage.
She's come
to take
my sister
away.

HOW DO YOU...

54815. 241.

How do you
know about
my fortune?
Do you think
my Dearest Goddess
would come
and give
my secret
away
so easily?

USE ME...

54824. 564.

Use me still,
Dearest Goddess,
find me
a place.
Put to shame
all those
who would
destroy
my good
name.

I SAW...

54832. 182.

I saw
the Dearest Goddess
hide among
the branches
of a blooming
linden tree.

When I got there,
she whispered:
don't you dare
pluck
my silken
tresses.

THE DAY...

58834. 389.

The day
I was born
the Dearest Goddess
faced three choices:
whether
I should die;
whether
I should live;
whether
I should
lose my mother
and become
an orphan.

I SAW...

I saw
the Dearest Goddess
come into
the church
with two virgins.
One virgin
carried
a golden chair;
the other
a book.

The moment
the Dearest Goddess
sat down
to read,
I saw
nails pop
from the cross,
and Jesus
rise
into heaven.

IN THE MIDDLE...

33738. 407. 134.

In the middle
of the sea
on a rock...

that's where
the Dearest Goddess
goes to gather
red berries,
red flowers,
and tears
shed by
the sun.

THE BIRCH...

33748. 190.

The birch
has only
three leaves.

Behind
the first leaf
the sun
rises;
behind
the second leaf
the sun
sets.
The Dearest Goddess
pours
pure silver
over
the third.

IF ONLY...

9203. 264.

If I only
knew
the path of
the Unwelcome Goddess,
I'd catch up
to her,
stuff
her sack
with
eggs
and
send her
up a mountain
of ice.

SAYS THE SUN...

33899. 156.

Says the sun
while setting:
the top
of the forest
is uneven.

Dearest Goddess,
take
your golden scissors,
even out
the tree
tops.

THE SONS...

33983. 88.

The sons
of the wind,
the daughters
of the sun,
together,
went bathing
in the sea.

They might have
drowned
but for
the Dearest Goddess,
their chaperone.

FOR THREE DAYS...

34015. 91.

For three days
and nights
the Dearest Goddess
and God
were at odds
with each other.

The Dearest Goddess
had bleached
her cloud linens
white.
Then God came
along
and turned them
grey.

THIS IS...

54935. 445.

This is
what I received
from
the Dearest Goddess.

A yard
surrounded
by linden trees;
a garden
of white poppies;
in the middle
spins
the sun.

SHUT UP, YOU...

55057. 373.

Shut up, you.
Do you know
who
you are
speaking to?

God is
my father,
the Dearest Goddess
is my mother,
and my brothers
and sisters
are not orphans.

TELL ME...

55290. 168.
55292. 605.

Tell me,
Dearest Goddess,
your dream.

Did you see
a sow
with horns,
a rooster
with teats,
a goat
bearing piglets?
Did you see
a fish
kiss
a fish?

THE BLOOD RIVER...

34108. 69.

The blood river
coils
and coils.
Come, hurry,
Dearest Goddess,
come,
ford the river,
learn
what blood is,
stop
the bleeding.

THE BEAVER...

55381.

The beaver
can swim
the river
and the sea.
The beaver
makes
his house
at the bottom
of the lake.
The beaver
raises children
who cannot
drown, nor
are they
lazy.
Dearest Goddess,
give me
the beaver's good
fortune.

THE WOLF...

55401. 406.

The wolf
bragged
and the bear
bragged
that they
are strong.

Dearest Goddess,
I left them
behind.
On my journey
I need
only your
company.

GIVE...

34185. 73.

Give,
Dearest Goddess,
what's
to be given.
I'll take
what's
to be taken
with both hands,
without
hesitation.

WHY SHOULDN'T...

3276. 30.
3283. 134.

Why shouldn't
I complain to
the Dearest Goddess?
My mother
seldom
praises me.

Still,
the Dearest Goddess
tells me:
it could be worse
—if in place
of my mother
I have to
depend
on strangers.

IF YOU WISH...

39406. 3.

If you wish
earnestly
for dignity,
the Dearest Goddess
will bring you
a wreath
of flowers.
If you don't
reach for it,
all you
may get
is a wreath
of thistles.

HERE I AM...

38633. 322.

Here I am
wishing to be
this,
wishing to be
that.
Before I dare
wish for more,
let me see
how
the Dearest Goddess
has endowed me.

DON'T BRING ME...

5282. 137.
5283. 91.   Don't bring me
sorrow,
Dearest Goddess.
Let the wind
take it away.
Give it,
if you must,
to the clucking hen.
She knows
how to
cluck on it.

I THANK...

5417. 127.
5699., 169.

I thank
the Dearest Goddess
and my mother.
The Dearest Goddess
gave me beauty,
my mother
supplied me
with the silk
and the gold.

WE ARE...

5568. 114.

We are
three sisters
with six
ripe teats.
Dearest Goddess,
we've come
to complain:
Where are
the boys?

BE MY HELPMATE...

5926. 86.

Be my helpmate,
Dearest Goddess.
Let the roses
I plant tonight
bloom into
a rose garden
by morning.

THOUGH...

6519. 16.

Though
we are not
sisters,
we call
ourselves
sisters.
It makes
some people
mad.
It makes
the Dearest Goddess
glad.

THE LEAVES...

39353. 241.

The leaves
of the linden
do not quake,
her daughters
do not hate.
Dearest Goddess,
all the world
weeps
if we don't
speak
peace.

THE DEAREST GODDESS...

6621. 191.
6622. 90.

The Dearest Goddess
is wondering
what to do
with this
daughter:
though she
spreads shame,
she hides
behind a wreath
of flowers.

If she doesn't
change for
the better,
I'll change
her flowers
into thorns.

I LOST...

5037. 290.   I lost
my mother
in the fog.
I walked
through
two birch groves
looking
for her.
In the third
grove,
I found
a silvery river
and two women
bathing.
One was
my mother,
the other
the Dearest Goddess.
My mother said:
go away.
The Dearest Goddess
said:
come here,
I'll give you
a handkerchief
to wipe away
those tears.

THE DEAREST GODDESS...

35817. 83

The Dearest Goddess
gave me
a thousand songs
at the tip
of every
wheel spoke.
Whenever
I'm sad,
all I need
to do
is turn
the wheel,
and song
flows.

THE UNWELCOME GODDESS...

44615. 327.   The Unwelcome Goddess
                     gave me
                     a present
                     of fancy shoes
                     for a party.

                     If you'll be
                     my chaperone,
                     Dearest Goddess,
                     I'll be happy
                     to dance
                     barefoot.

LOVERS...

11871. 104.

Lovers,
don't tryst
in the birch grove.
That's where
the Dearest Goddess
sleeps
under
a sheet
of green silk.

HOW SHALL I...

6862 (22874)   How shall I
make peace?
Dearest God,
will you
give me
understanding?
Dearest Goddess,
will you
give me
advice?

The Singer

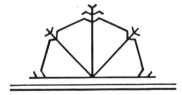

SISTER, DON'T SING...

36446. 605
36453. 241

Sister, don't sing
only half the song.
People will speak
and say
you cannot complete
the jobs
you have
in hand.
They'll say
you're always
ailing.

I DON'T MAKE...

35802. 224.   I don't make
my song;
I only sing it.
I sing my song
with words
given to me by
the Dearest Goddess.

IT'S EASY...

36508. 127.   It's easy
to sing
when the flowers
bloom,
during the summer
when the weather
is clear.
It takes a nightingale,
however,
to sing
a happy song
in a dry pine.

IT'S...

36524. 170.   It's
as it should be:
I was born
where the birds
make their nest;
I found
my name
at a country fair.
Whenever I sing
the mountains
echo.

WHAT'S WRONG...

36562. 443.   What's wrong
with my man?
He's out barking
with the dogs.
I'm smarter.
I walk
singing.

I WASTE...

36577. 241.   I waste
                   my song here.
                   Haven't you heard?
                   The women here
                   want to lick out
                   the pan
                   before inviting me
                   into
                   the house.

WHEN I SING...

22. *156.*   When I sing
                    I sing happily;
                    when I cry
                    I shed a river
                    of tears.
                    I learnt my song
                    from the Dearest Goddess;
                    I learnt my tears
                    being an orphan.

WE HAVE SUNG...

22. 6. 379.   We have sung
                every song
                we can
                think of.
                Where
                can we find more?
                Let's go visit
                the song closet
                of our twin sisters:
                there
                no sooner
                the one writes them,
                the other passes
                the song along
                singing.

MY MOTHER...

4. 115.
10. 290.

My mother
died singing,
and so
did my father.
So will I.
And after I die,
I will go on
singing
with my sister
from the top
of our graves.

UNHAPPY PEOPLE...

57. 26.
59. 195.
103. 405

Unhappy people
will not
get me down.
As soon
as I
can get away,
I'll sing and dance
again.

But do you know
what will stop
a song?
A slap in the face,
a fist in the back.
Else, I will sing
even through tears.

MY MOTHER...

97. 16
35874. 286   My mother
              raised me
              in a nightingale's
              nest.
              I grew up
              to sing
              with a nightingale's
              tongue,
              to hear
              my songs
              roll the echo
              from the mountain
              down through
              the valley.

COME, SWEET...

294. 137.   Come, Sweet,
sing with me.
If you sing well,
I'll stick with you.
Come, let us prove
we can sing
in such harmony
that
we'll squeeze out
even the water
between us.

MY THROAT...

My throat
is like
a trumpet—
I can compete
even with brass.
My voice
is like gold
and flows
even
through
hard rock.

FINLAND

BALTIC
SEA

ESTONIA

LATVIA

LITHUANIA

POLAND

Eso Benjamins is an artist and writer living in the metropolitan Washington area. He was born in Latvia and moved to the United States after World War II. His interest in Latvian folklore dates back to the war years, which he spent living in rural Latvia.